Cook's Dessert Cookbook

Cook's Dessert Cookbook

An Angie Amalfi Mysteries Cookbook

JOANNE PENCE

with Illustrations by
LORETTA BARRA

QUAIL HILL PUBLISHING

Any references to historical events, real people, or real locales are used fictitiously. Other names, characters, places and incidents are the product of the author's imagination, and any resemblance to actual events, locales or persons, living or dead, is entirely coincidental.

No part of this book may be reproduced or transmitted in any form or by any electronic or mechanical means including information storage and retrieval systems without permission in writing from the author, except by a reviewer who may quote brief passages in a review. This book may not be resold or uploaded for distribution to others.

Quail Hill Publishing
PO Box 64
Eagle, ID 83616

Visit our website at www.quailhillpublishing.net

First Quail Hill Publishing Paperback Printing: September 2016
Second Quail Hill Publishing Paperback Printing: August 2018
First Quail Hill E-book: September 2016

Copyright © 2016 Joanne Pence
Illustrations copyright © 2016 Loretta Barra
All rights reserved.

ISBN-13: 978-1-949566-34-5

*This cookbook was created by two sisters to keep alive
the wonderful recipes of our mother and grandmother
(and some of our own favorites), and with the hope
that our children and grandchildren will use
these recipes to carry on the
traditions of our family.*

PREFACE

Spatula-wielding crime-fighter Angie Amalfi burst upon the literary scene nearly twenty-five years ago in a mystery called *Something's Cooking*.

The Angie Amalfi mysteries continue to this day with all the usual suspects—Angie and the love of her life, San Francisco Homicide Inspector Paavo Smith; her best friend, Connie Rogers; her annoying neighbor, Stan Bonnette; and her large Italian family—playing major roles in these stories of crime and cooking. You'll find everyone mentioned in the recipes that follow.

More than anything, Angie loves desserts (as do I, and as does my sister, Loretta Barra, who painted the watercolors used in the book). This cookbook is a compendium of dessert recipes from Angie's mysteries as well as a number of our family favorites.

We hope you'll enjoy making the desserts presented here. And afterward, treat yourself by curling up in a comfortable chair with some freshly baked goodies by your side, and an Angie Amalfi mystery in your hands.

Buon appetito!

--Joanne Pence

CONTENTS

Something Italian — 13

Angie's Easy Tiramisu — 14
Cannoli — 16
Italian Napoleons — 18
Ossi Di Morti Cookies (Bones of the Dead) — 21
Italian Style Chocolate-Amaretto Bread Pudding — 22
Lite Chocolate Amaretto Cheesecake — 24
Iced Italian Wedding Cookies — 26
Biscotti di Prato (Tuscan Almond Biscotti) — 29
Orange-Cinnamon Biscotti — 32
Zabaglione — 34
Italian Cheese Pie — 36
Italian Honey Cookies — 39
Zeppole — 40

Something Special — 41

Chocolate Soufflé — 42
French Macarons — 44
Greek Butter Cookies (Kourabiedes) — 48

Snickerdoodles	49
Ultimate Cheesecake	51
Chocolate Rum Cake	53
Christmas Vanilla Horns	54
Almond Marzipan Candies	56
Chocolate Éclairs	58
Floating Islands	61
Pumpkin Pie with Praline Topping	63
Cocoa Sauerkraut Cake	65
Easy Petit Fours	67

Something Fruit-filled   70

Cranberry Cream Scones	71
Peach Kuchen	73
Mom's Apple Pie	74
Best Lemon Squares Ever	76
Pineapple-Cherry Dreams	78
Chewy Chocolate-Cherry Cookies	81
Skinny Fig Bars	83
Lemon Meringue Tart with Gingersnap Crust	85
Lite Lemon Bread Pudding & Blackberry Sauce	88
Cherry Coconut Birthday Cupcakes	89

Exquisite Raspberry Tart	91
Chocolate Torte with Apricot Filling	94

Something Nutty   97

Almond Praline Meringue Layer Cake	98
Almond Butter Cake with Crunchy Almond Topping	102
Mocha Pecan Torte	103
Pistachio Pudding Bars	105
Linzer Torte	107
Bourbon Pecan Chocolate Pie	110
Zucchini Bread	111
Heavenly Carrot-Walnut Cake & Cream Cheese Frosting.	112
Almond Divinity Candy	115
Cardamom Icebox Cookies	116
Almond Rose Cookies	117
"Hello Dolly" Cookies	120

Something Italian

Angie's Easy Tiramisu

The literal translation of "tiramisu" is "pull me up." Whether this derives from the caffeine content of the coffee and chocolate, or from the liqueur, is anybody's guess. Angie loves to serve this creamy dessert after a nice Italian meal.

Ingredients:
3/4 cup brewed espresso coffee (or triple-strength regular coffee), cooled
1/4-1/2 cup liqueur (brandy or rum is most often used)
24 (or more) ladyfinger cookies (hard ones work best)
4 eggs, separated
1/4 cup granulated sugar
1 pound mascarpone cheese (do not use cream cheese as a substitute)
6 ounces (or more) semisweet chocolate, grated.

Directions:
Combine the cooled coffee with the liqueur. Arrange 12 or more of the ladyfingers in a flat-bottomed serving dish with high sides, covering the entire bottom of the dish. Sprinkle or *lightly* soak the ladyfingers with half of the liqueur/coffee mixture.

In a small bowl, beat egg whites until stiff. Set them aside.

In another bowl, beat the egg yolks with the sugar until the mixture thickens and turns light in color. Stir in the mascarpone to combine thoroughly. Gently fold the egg whites into this mixture. Spread half the mascarpone mixture over the ladyfingers in the serving dish. Sprinkle half the grated chocolate on top of the mascarpone mixture. Be generous with the chocolate—you might need more than 6 ounces depending on the size of your serving dish. You should be able to still see the mascarpone below, but make sure the mixture is fairly well covered.

On a separate plate, lightly soak the remaining ladyfingers with the remaining coffee/liqueur mixture and use them to create another layer of ladyfingers on top of the chopped chocolate. Add the rest of the mascarpone on top of the lady fingers, and then add the rest of the grated chocolate.

Cover the tiramisu with plastic wrap and chill overnight, or for at least 5 hours. Serves 6-8.

Cannoli

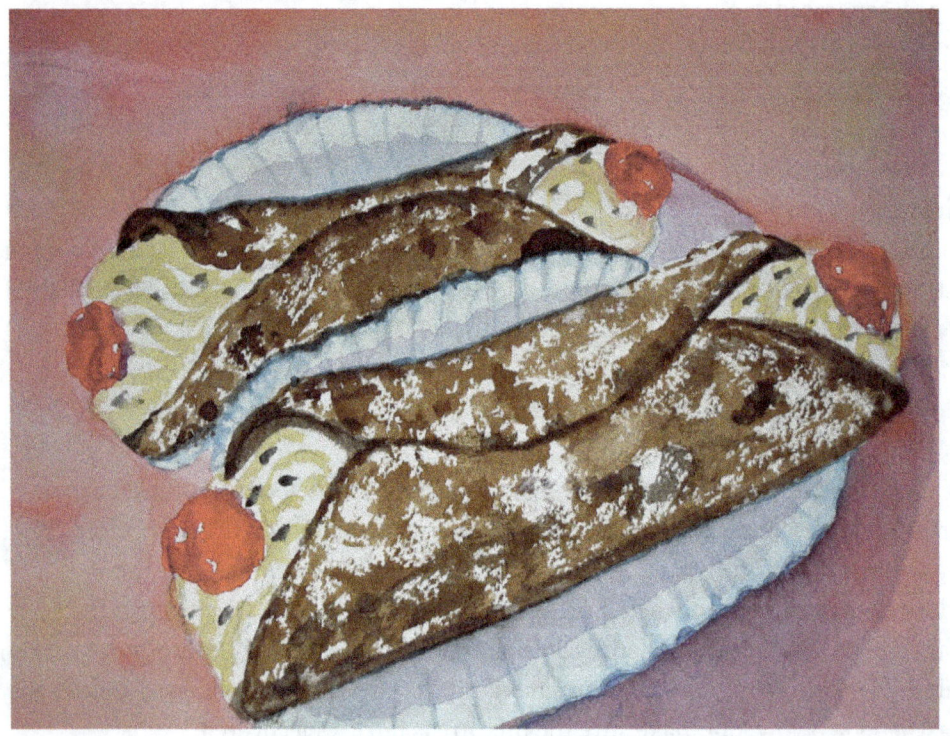

"Don't forget the cannoli," is one of Angie's favorite lines from *The Godfather* movie. She never forgets the cannoli. Here's a simple recipe for you to make your own, using store bought cannoli pastry shells.

Ingredients:
1 pint part-skim ricotta cheese
1 cup confectioners' sugar
1/2 cup blanched slivered almonds
1/3 cup mini semi-sweet chocolate chips
1 tablespoon amaretto liqueur*
12 cannoli shells
1 tablespoon confectioners' sugar
1 tablespoon unsweetened cocoa powder
12 maraschino cherries

Directions:
Stir ricotta cheese with sugar in a large bowl. Mix thoroughly. Add almonds, chocolate chips and amaretto. Stir to combine.

Carefully spoon into cannoli shells (or pipe from a pastry bag), filling from the center out. Put a maraschino cherry into filling on each end of each cannoli. Sprinkle cannoli with powdered sugar and cocoa.

*Note: 1/8 teaspoon almond extract mixed with 1 tablespoon water can be substituted for the almond liqueur.

Italian Napoleons

Every year at Christmas time, Angie's mother buys these pastries at an Italian bakery shop in the North Beach section of San Francisco. But throughout the year Angie likes to make an "easy" version of a Napoleon. Rather than using the traditional puff pastry she uses phyllo dough brushed with butter. They turn out every bit as flaky as the originals.

Preheat oven to 375°

Ingredients:

3/4 cup whole milk
2 egg yolks
1/4 cup granulated sugar
1 tablespoon flour
1-1/2 teaspoon rum or rum extract
9 sheets frozen phyllo pastry, thawed
1/3 cup heavy cream
4 tablespoons unsalted butter, melted
2 tablespoons confectioners' sugar
Seedless raspberry jam

Directions for Custard Filling:

In a saucepan bring 1/2 cup milk to a boil. In a small bowl, whisk the remaining 1/4 cup milk with egg yolks and sugar, when combined, add flour and continue to whisk until smooth. Drizzle in a small amount of the hot milk into the egg yolk mixture, stir, and then add the egg yolk mixture into the saucepan with the milk.

Cook over medium heat, stirring constantly, until thick and mixture just comes to a boil. Reduce the heat and cook 2 more minutes stirring constantly. Remove from heat then stir in the rum. Pour into small bowl, cover the surface of the filling with plastic wrap and cool to room temperature. Refrigerate it for at least an hour (until cold).

Directions for Building Napoleons:

Coat a 15"x10"x1" inch jelly roll pan with nonstick cooking spray. Spread one pastry phyllo sheet on the prepared pan. Brush that sheet with melted butter. Repeat layering all nine phyllo sheets with butter. With a sharp knife cut the sheets lengthwise into thirds. Cover with nonstick foil and another baking pan. Bake at 375 degrees for 15 to 18 minutes or until the pastry layers brown. Remove top pan and foil and let cool.

In a small bowl beat the heavy cream to stiff peaks. Stir the cold custard and then gently fold it into the 1/3 cup heavy cream. Place one pastry strip on a cutting board. Spread a thin layer of raspberry jam and then half of the custard onto the pastry. Top with a second pastry strip then gently spread a thin layer of raspberry jam and then with remaining custard. Top with final pastry strip and dust with powdered sifted sugar and raspberries or cherries for decoration. Slice into pieces with a sharp serrated knife. Serve within 2 hours of layering. Makes 6 servings

Ossi Di Morti Cookies (Bones of the Dead)

Angie likes to make these cookies as a Halloween treat. In Italy, they're traditionally made around All Souls' Day (November 2nd; the day after All Saint's Day). Angie's family loves the way they're crunchy on the outside,
and airy inside

Preheat oven to 375°
Ingredients:
3 eggs
2 cups powdered sugar
2 cups flour
1 teaspoon baking powder

Directions:
In a large bowl, beat eggs on high speed for 5 to 6 minutes. Slowly add sugar and continue to beat the eggs, about another 5 minutes more. Mix flour and baking powder together. Add them, 1/3 at a time, to egg mixture.

On a floured work board, roll dough into long pieces about 1-1/2 inches thick, and 10-12 inches long. If dough is too sticky, add more flour. Cover and let sit overnight (you might want to place them on a cookie sheet for this).

Next day, again place dough on floured surface. Cut in bits 1 1/2 inches long. Place the bits on a cookie sheet and lightly squeeze the center so that it's more narrow than the ends (bone shaped, in other words). Or, if you want to be more elaborate, with scissors or a sharp knife, you can make a small cut on each end so each tip of the cookie looks like a small "Y."

Bake 20 minutes until light golden brown. remove and allow to cool.

Italian Style Chocolate-Amaretto Bread Pudding

Even people who aren't particularly fond of bread pudding sit up and take notice when Angie makes this dessert. It's bread pudding with an Italian twist.

Preheat oven to 350°

Ingredients for Bread Pudding:

1-1/2 pound loaf panettone bread (if none available, use a sweet French bread or challah) trim crust & cut into 1-inch cubes
1 cup chocolate chips
8 large eggs
1-1/2 cups whipping cream
2-1/2 cups whole milk
1 cup sugar
2 tablespoons amaretto liqueur

Ingredients for Amaretto Sauce:

1/2 cup whipping cream
1/2 cup whole milk
3 tablespoons sugar
1/4 cup amaretto liqueur
2 teaspoons cornstarch

Directions for Bread Pudding:

Lightly butter a 13"x9"x2" baking dish. Put bread cubes evenly in pan, then sprinkle chocolate chips over them, spreading evenly.

In a large bowl, add eggs, cream, milk, sugar, and amaretto, then whisk until blended. Pour the custard over the bread cubes and chocolate. Press the bread cubes gently to be sure they're all submerged. Let stand for at least 30 minutes, occasionally pressing the bread again into the custard mixture. (Can let stand up to 2 hours; but if much over 30 minutes, cover and refrigerate.)

Bake until the pudding is set in the center, about 1 hour. While the pudding is in the oven, make the amaretto sauce:

Directions for Sauce:
Using a heavy, small saucepan, add cream, milk, and sugar. Over medium heat, bring to boil, stirring frequently. Mix amaretto and cornstarch in small bowl, stir to mix and break up any cornstarch lumps. Stir amaretto-cornstarch into the cream mixture. Simmer over medium-low heat until the sauce thickens, stirring constantly, about 2 minutes. Set aside and keep warm. (If made ahead, store in refrigerator, and warm in microwave before serving.)

Putting it all together . . .
When the pudding is cooked, allow it to cool slightly, and then spoon the bread pudding into bowls, drizzle it with the warm amaretto sauce, and serve. While the pudding is best served warm, if prepared early, it can be reheated in the microwave before serving.

Lite Chocolate Amaretto Cheesecake

This is a lighter version of the cheesecake that Angie makes for Paavo. Angie and her best friend, Connie Rogers, enjoy this dessert because it tastes rich, despite having fewer calories than most cheesecakes. They enjoy it with a cup of dark espresso coffee.

Preheat oven to 300 °

Ingredients:

6 chocolate wafers, finely crushed

1-1/2 cups light process cream cheese

1 cup sugar

1 cup 1% low-fat cottage cheese

1/4 cup plus 2 tablespoons unsweetened cocoa

1/4 cup all-purpose flour

1/4 cup amaretto

1 teaspoon salt

1 egg

2 tablespoons semi-sweet chocolate mini-morsels

Chocolate shards (optional - as garnish for top of cake)

1 cup raspberries dipped in sugar (optional – for top of cake)

Directions:

Press chocolate wafer crumbs to bottom of a 8-inch springform pan.

In a bowl add cream cheese, sugar, cottage cheese, cocoa, flour, amaretto and salt. Using a mixer or food processor, blend until smooth. Add egg and mix until blended then fold in the semi-sweet chocolate morsels.

Pour this mixture over the chocolate cookie crumbs in the spring-form pan. Bake at 300 degrees for 45-50 minutes or until cheesecake is set.

Let cool then cover and refrigerate for at least 8 hours.

Remove the sides of the pan and transfer the cheesecake to a serving plate. Garnish with shards of chocolate and raspberries that are dipped in sugar.

Iced Italian Wedding Cookies

Angie's mother, Serefina, often makes these for weddings and at Easter time. They are round, or S-shaped and iced with thin pastel-colored icing. When Angie was a little girl she made these cookies with her mother and sprinkled multicolored nonpareils on them before the icing hardened.

Preheat oven to 375°

Cookie Ingredients:

1/2 lb. butter (2 cubes), softened
1 cup sugar
2 large eggs, beaten
2 teaspoons vanilla extract
1 teaspoon almond extract
3-1/2 cups flour (may need more depending on dough)
2 tablespoons baking powder

Icing Ingredients:

1-3/4 cup powdered sugar
1 tablespoon vanilla extract
2 tablespoons milk
Food coloring of your choice (pink, yellow, light green are commonly used)
Nonpareils (tiny little ball shaped colorful sprinkles)

Directions:

In a large bowl, use mixer to cream butter and sugar until fluffy. Add beaten eggs, vanilla and almond flavorings and mix well. Combine flour and baking powder. Slowly add flour to butter mixture. Beat slowly. If the dough becomes too thick for your mixer, add the remaining flour by hand.

Using one tablespoon of dough for each cookie, on a lightly floured surface, roll the dough into a cylinder and then form it into a circle, S-shape, braids, or bows. (Add more flour if the dough is too soft to hold its shape.)

Bake at 375 degrees until lightly browned around 15 minutes.

Icing – Mix powered sugar, vanilla extract, and milk to form a thin icing (add more sugar if the icing is too thin; more milk if too thick). If you would like different colors of icing, divide the icing into bowls and add a few drops of food coloring to each bowl to lightly tint the icing.

When the cookies cool, ice them and immediately sprinkle the icing with nonpareils before the icing sets.

Biscotti di Prato (Tuscan Almond Biscotti)

Angie likes to bake these cookies to have with coffee when her neighbor Stan drops by…which is quite often. "Biscotti" means "twice baked" which makes these cookies very crunchy—perfect for dunking in coffee or enjoyed with an after dinner wine. They keep quite a while in an airtight tin.

Preheat oven 350°

Ingredients:
3-1/4 cups unbleached all-purpose flour
2 cups sugar
1 teaspoon double-acting baking powder
1/4 teaspoon salt
4 large whole eggs
2 large egg yolks
1 teaspoon vanilla extract
1/2 teaspoon almond extract
1-3/4 cups blanched whole almonds, lightly toasted and coarsely chopped
An egg wash made by beating together 1 large egg and 1 teaspoon water

Directions:
In a large bowl add flour, sugar, baking powder and salt, stir until well blended.

In a small bowl, use a mixer or whisk and beat together the 4 whole eggs, 2 egg yolks, vanilla and almond extract. Slowly add the egg mix to the flour mixture, and beat until completely blended. Stir in the almonds.

On a lightly floured surface knead the dough several times. Divide it in quarters. With floured hands form each quarter into a flattish log 12-inches long and 2-inches wide. Place the logs at least 3 inches apart on 2 large buttered and floured baking sheets. Brush the logs with the egg wash.

Bake for 35 minutes then let cool on the baking sheets for 10 minutes.

Place logs on cutting board and cut crosswise on the diagonal into 3/4-inch thick slices. Makes about 56 biscotti. Arrange the cookies, cut sides down, on the baking sheets and bake them for 5-6 minutes on each side, until they turn golden brown.

Biscotti di Prato (Tuscan Almond Biscotti)

Angie likes to bake these cookies to have with coffee when her neighbor Stan drops by…which is quite often. "Biscotti" means "twice baked" which makes these cookies very crunchy—perfect for dunking in coffee or enjoyed with an after dinner wine. They keep quite a while in an airtight tin.

Preheat oven 350°

Ingredients:
3-1/4 cups unbleached all-purpose flour
2 cups sugar
1 teaspoon double-acting baking powder
1/4 teaspoon salt
4 large whole eggs
2 large egg yolks
1 teaspoon vanilla extract
1/2 teaspoon almond extract
1-3/4 cups blanched whole almonds, lightly toasted and coarsely chopped
An egg wash made by beating together 1 large egg and 1 teaspoon water

Directions:
In a large bowl add flour, sugar, baking powder and salt, stir until well blended.

In a small bowl, use a mixer or whisk and beat together the 4 whole eggs, 2 egg yolks, vanilla and almond extract. Slowly add the egg mix to the flour mixture, and beat until completely blended. Stir in the almonds.

On a lightly floured surface knead the dough several times. Divide it in quarters. With floured hands form each quarter into a flattish log 12-inches long and 2-inches wide. Place the logs at least 3 inches apart on 2 large buttered and floured baking sheets. Brush the logs with the egg wash.

Bake for 35 minutes then let cool on the baking sheets for 10 minutes.

Place logs on cutting board and cut crosswise on the diagonal into 3/4-inch thick slices. Makes about 56 biscotti. Arrange the cookies, cut sides down, on the baking sheets and bake them for 5-6 minutes on each side, until they turn golden brown.

Cool the biscotti on cookie racks. Store in airtight cookie tins.

Orange-Cinnamon Biscotti

Since Angie adores biscotti, here's a second biscotti recipe.

Preheat oven to 350°

Ingredients:
4 eggs
1-1/4 cups plus 2 tablespoons sugar
3/4 cup canola oil
1/4 cup orange juice
1 tablespoon grated orange peel
1 teaspoon vanilla extract
4 cups all-purpose flour
2 teaspoons baking powder
1/2 teaspoon salt
1 cup cinnamon chips (Hershey's® or similar)
2 teaspoons ground cinnamon

Directions:
In large bowl, add eggs, only 1 cup of the sugar, oil, orange juice, orange peel, and vanilla. Beat 2 minutes at medium speed.

In medium bowl, stir together flour, the remaining 1/4 cup of sugar, baking powder, and salt.

At low speed add flour mixture into the egg mixture, a bit at a time, until just blended. Stir in cinnamon chips. (Dough will be sticky.) Refrigerate 30 minutes.

Line baking sheet with parchment or use non-stick spray on it. Then, with floured hands, shape dough into four logs, each about 2 inches wide. Place on baking sheet.

Bake 25-30 minutes until light brown. Remove from oven and let cool slightly.

On small plate, stir together 2 tablespoons of sugar and ground cinnamon. Cut logs into pieces 1/2-inch wide. Dip both sides of each biscotti into cinnamon mixture. Return to baking sheet. Bake 6-8 minutes or until light golden brown. Cool completely. Makes about 40 cookies.

Zabaglione

Zabaglione is a traditional Italian dessert usually served warm, spooned into glasses or served over sliced fruit or with plain cake. Try this recipe with whipped cream and chocolate!

Ingredients:
6 egg yolks
3/4 cup sugar
1 cup Marsala wine
1 cup heavy cream
1 ounce semisweet chocolate

Directions:
First prepare whipped cream: beat cream until it forms stiff peaks. Refrigerate.

In small bowl, stir egg yolks and sugar until soft and foamy, about 3-5 minutes. Slowly add Marsala, stirring constantly. Place mixture in top of a double boiler and place it over gently simmering (not boiling) water. Whisk continuously as custard mixture cooks. It will foam, and then swell into a soft mass. When it thickens enough to retain a slight peak when the whisk is withdrawn (about 5-8 minutes), remove it from the heat.

Spoon a little cold whipped cream onto bottom of stemmed glasses. Top with hot zabaglione.   Garnish with semisweet chocolate curls.

Makes 6-8 servings.

Italian Cheese Pie

The first time Angie went to Italy with her family, she had a piece of Italian Cheese Pie in Florence. Now every time she bakes it, she is flooded with memories of that wonderful trip. She is looking forward to taking Paavo there someday.

Preheat oven to 350°

Crust Ingredients:

1-1/2 cups unsifted all-purpose flour
1-1/4 teaspoons baking powder
1/2 teaspoon salt
3 tablespoons butter, softened
1/4 cup sugar
1 egg
1/2 teaspoon vanilla extract
1/2 teaspoon freshly grated orange peel
1 tablespoon orange juice
1 egg, separated (to be used at very end to brush crust)

Filling Ingredients:

1 container ricotta cheese (15 oz.)
3/4 cup sugar
3 eggs
1-1/2 teaspoons flour
1 teaspoon almond extract
2 tablespoons finely chopped citron (or if you prefer, 2 tablespoons mini semi-sweet chocolate chips)

Directions for Crust:

Sift flour with baking powder and salt. With electric mixer, beat butter, sugar and one egg in a medium bowl until fluffy. Beat in vanilla, orange peel and orange juice. Add half of the flour mixture and beat until blended. Add remaining flour mixture, mixing with hands until dough leaves side of bowl and holds together. Cover in plastic wrap and set aside.

Directions for Filling:

Beat ricotta cheese until creamy. Add sugar, 3 eggs, flour, almond extract and beat until well blended. Stir in citron or chocolate chips.

Putting it all together:
Divide pastry dough in half. On moistened surface, roll half of dough between two sheets of waxed paper to an 11-inch circle. Remove top paper and fit pastry into a 9-inch pie plate. Trim the excess pastry. Brush the bottom of the pastry with egg white.

Roll remaining half of pastry to 1/8 inch thickness. Cut into ten strips, each about 1/2-inch wide.

Spoon the ricotta filling into the pastry pie crust. Lattice topping by placing five (5) pastry strips across filling, pressing firmly to edge of pie plate. Then place the remaining five (5) pastry strips across the first ones.

Press the tines of a fork firmly along the edge of the pie/lattice crusts along the rim of the pie pan. Remove and discard any of the lattice that hangs over the edge of the pan.

Beat egg yolk with one tablespoon of water and brush over crust.

Place a strip of foil around edge of pie crust to prevent overbrowning. Bake 50 minutes, or until top is golden-brown and filling is set.

Cool in refrigerator 8 hours or overnight.

Italian Honey Cookies

Angie's grandmother often made a big batch of these cookies—they keep a long time, and harden as they age. Angie always enjoyed dunking them in milk when she was a child. Now, when no one's looking, she dunks them in strong coffee.

Preheat oven to 350°
Ingredients:
1 cup milk
2 eggs
1/2 cup oil
2 cups honey
5 cups flour
2 teaspoons baking powder

Directions:
In a large bowl add milk, eggs, oil, and honey. Using an electric mixer, beat until well combined. Slowly add 4 (not 5) cups of flour and baking powder. If mixture is still wet, continue to add flour until it feels fairly dry. You'll need to mix it by hand at that point.

For each cookie, take 2-3 teaspoons of dough, roll it into a cylinder, and then shape it into an "S" or a circle.

Bake at 350 degrees 12 minutes or so until browned. Lay the cookies out on cooling racks and store them almost immediately in an airtight container. Some people add a slice of apple to the container to keep the cookies for turning hard—but many other people prefer the cookies when they turn hard. Try them both ways!

Angie's great-grandmother made these "Italian" doughnuts

Ingredients:
vegetable oil for frying
1 cup all-purpose flour
2 teaspoons baking soda
1 pinch of salt
1/4 cup white sugar
2 eggs, beaten
1 cup ricotta cheese
1 teaspoon vanilla extract
1/2 cup confectioners' sugar for dusting

Directions:
Pour about two inches of oil into deep-fryer or large saucepan and heat to 375 degrees F.

Combine flour, baking soda, salt and sugar in medium bowl. Stir in the eggs, ricotta cheese and vanilla. The batter will be thick and sticky.

Drop by tablespoonful into the hot oil. Cook 3 or 4 at a time. Fry about 2 minutes, flip them over, and continue to fry until golden brown another 1 or 2 minutes (3 to 4 minutes total).

Place on paper towels to absorb excess oil, and then dust with confectioners' sugar.

Best served warm.

Something Special

Chocolate Soufflé

Angie makes this as a "Special Occasion Dessert" ... such as on Valentine's Day! The following recipe is surprisingly easy—simple enough, in fact, that Angie can whip it up while she's helping Paavo solve a murder mystery.

Preheat oven 350°

Ingredients:
3 tablespoons butter
3 tablespoons flour
1 cup milk
1/2 cup sugar
3 squares (3 ounces) melted, unsweetened chocolate
4 egg yolks
1 teaspoons vanilla
5 egg whites
1/4 teaspoon cream of tartar

Directions:
In a saucepan over low heat, melt the butter and then blend in flour. Slowly stir in the milk and sugar until the sauce thickens and forms little bubbles. Add the melted chocolate. Turn off the heat, cover the saucepan and cool until the mixture is lukewarm.

Once the mixture is cool, mix in egg yolks and vanilla. Beat the egg whites with cream of tartar until stiff but not dry. Slowly fold 1/4 of the egg whites into the chocolate mixture. Once that is done, gently fold the rest of the egg whites into the chocolate mixture.

Tie a 3-inch high foil or parchment collar around the top of a 1-1/2 quart soufflé dish. Spoon the soufflé gently into the dish. Smooth the top and run a groove about 1/2-inch deep around the outer edge, and about 1-1/2 inches in from the sides.

Bake at 350 degrees for 40 to 45 minutes until puffed up and browned.

Serve immediately with sprinkled powdered sugar or a dollop of whipped cream. Serves four.

French Macarons

The first time Angie heard of these cookies she thought her sister, Caterina, was talking about "macaroons" but pronouncing them weirdly. Then, when Caterina brought her some of these delicate "sandwich" cookies from Paris, Angie was hooked! They are heavenly. They do take time to make but macaron lovers find it worth every minute. Give yourself a couple of hours so you can have fun with the cookies as you try out a variety of colors and fillings.

Preheat oven to 300°

Ingredients:
1-3/4 cups confectioners' sugar
1 cup almond flour
3 large egg whites (at room temperature)
1/4 teaspoon cream of tartar
Pinch of salt
1/4 cup superfine sugar
2 to 3 drops of gel food coloring (your choice of color)
1/2 teaspoon vanilla, almond or mint extract
Assorted fillings (see below)

Directions:
Line 3 baking sheets with silicone mats.

In a bowl whisk the confectioners' sugar with almond flour to combine. Sift the sugar-almond flour mixture into a large bowl a little at a time through a fine mesh sieve.

Beat the room temperature egg whites, cream of tartar and salt on medium speed until frothy. Gradually add the superfine sugar and beat at a higher speed until the mixture turns stiff and shiny. It should take about 5 minutes.

Add the beaten egg white mix to the bowl with the almond flour mixture. Fold in the egg mix until it is incorporated with the flour.

Add the food coloring and extract. Continue folding and scraping down the bowl until the batter is smooth (2-3 minutes).

Transfer the batter into a pastry bag fitted with a 1/4- inch round tip. Hold the bag vertically but close to the silicone mat covered baking sheet and pipe 1-1/4 inch circles. Pipe 24 per baking sheet.

Firmly tap the baking sheets twice against the counter to release air bubbles. Let the cookies sit at room temperature until the tops are no longer sticky to the touch (from 15 minutes to 1 hour depending on the day's humidity).
Unless your baking sheets have thick bottoms, you should place an empty baking sheet beneath the sheet with the cookie dough. That will protect the bottom of the cookies from becoming too hot and scorched as they bake.

Bake the first batch about 20 minutes until the cookies are shiny and rise 1/8 inch to form a "foot." Transfer cookies to a wire rack to cool completely. Repeat with each baking sheet.

Peel the cookies off the mats and use two to create "sandwiches" with a thin layer of filling. See suggested fillings:

Cookie and Filling Ideas

Almond-Raspberry
Tint cookie batter with 2 drops pink gel food coloring. Flavor with Almond Extract. Fill with seedless raspberry jam.

Lavender-Honey
Tint cookie batter with 2 drops violet gel food coloring. Flavor with almond or vanilla extract. For the filling mix 3/4 cup mascarpone cheese, 2 tablespoons honey and 1 teaspoon ground dried lavender.

Mint-Chocolate
Tint the batter with 2 drops mint green gel food coloring. Flavor with mint extract. For the filling, microwave 3 ounces semi-sweet chocolate chips, 2 tablespoons heavy cream and 1 tablespoon butter, stirring until smooth.

Lemon
Tint cookie batter with 2 drops yellow food coloring. Use lemon curd as the filling

mix. (Angie calls these macarons her "Limoncello Treats.")

Be creative and make any cookie and filling combos you desire.

Greek Butter Cookies (Kourabiedes)

Angie loves a good, plain cookie that can be enjoyed with a cup of strong coffee. This is one such cookie.

Preheat oven to 400°
Ingredients:
1 cup butter, softened
3/4 cup white sugar
1 egg
1/2 teaspoon vanilla extract
1/2 teaspoon almond extract
2-1/4 cups all-purpose flour
1/2 cup confectioners' sugar

Directions:
In a medium bowl, cream together the butter, sugar, and egg until smooth. Stir in the vanilla and almond extracts. Gradually add in the flour to form the dough—you may have to knead it in by hand when it is too thick for a mixer or processor. Take about a teaspoon of dough at a time and roll it into a ball (then flatten a bit), a log, or an "S" shape.

Place cookies 1 to 2 inches apart onto cookie sheets prepared with non-stick spray or lightly greased with butter. Bake for 10 minutes, or until lightly browned and firm. Allow cookies to cool before dusting with confectioners' sugar.

These are often served in paper cupcake cups.

Snickerdoodles

These cookies were mentioned in Angie's first mystery adventure, *Something's Cooking*. Angie always enjoyed them at Christmas ... or any other time of the year, come to think of it.

Preheat oven to 375°
Ingredients:
1 cup butter
2 eggs
1-1/3 cups sugar
3 cups all-purpose flour
1 teaspoon baking soda
1-1/2 teaspoon cream of tartar
Pinch of salt
2 tablespoons sugar
1-1/2 teaspoon cinnamon

Directions:
In a large bowl, beat together butter, eggs and 1-1/3 cups of sugar until fluffy. Add flour, baking soda, cream of tartar, and salt, beating until blended. Shape into 1-inch balls.

Combine the 2 tablespoons of sugar and cinnamon in a small bowl. Mix thoroughly. Roll each cookie in the bowl, covering it with the Cinnamon-Sugar coating. Place each cookie about 2-1/2 inches apart on ungreased baking sheets.

Bake 10 minutes or until golden.

Remove cookies from baking sheets and cool on racks.

Ultimate Cheesecake

Very rich, dense, and delicious cheesecake—perfect for large parties. The following recipe makes one large 9"x13" or two 8" round cheesecakes.

Preheat oven to 350°

Ingredients for Crust:

4 cups graham cracker crumbs

4 tablespoons sugar

3 teaspoons cinnamon

6 tablespoons melted butter

Ingredients for Filling:

1-1/2 pounds (three 8 oz. packages) cream cheese, softened

1 cup sugar

4 well beaten eggs

2 teaspoons vanilla

Ingredients for Topping:

3 cups sour cream

7 teaspoons sugar

2 teaspoons vanilla

1/2 teaspoon almond extract

Directions for Crust:

Mix all the ingredients together then press the mixture into two 8" springform pans or one large 9"x13" casserole pan.

Directions for Filling:

Mix softened cream cheese, sugar, eggs and vanilla. Pour mixture into crust and bake 18 minutes at 350 degrees.

Directions for Topping:

Turn oven up to 375 degrees. Mix the ingredients together until smooth. Pour on top of cheesecake and bake for 10 minutes. Cool and refrigerate.

Chocolate Rum Cake

Here is a twist on the Italian Rum Cake Angie's family always enjoyed--an easy and quick cake to make for any occasion.

Preheat oven to 350°

Ingredients for Cake:

1 package of chocolate cake mix
1 package of chocolate instant pudding (4 serving size)
4 eggs
1/2 cup dark rum
1/2 cup cold water
1/2 cup vegetable oil

Ingredients for Filling:

1-1/2 cups cold milk
1/2 cup dark rum
1 package of chocolate instant pudding (4 serving size)
1 envelope whipped topping mix

Directions for Cake:

In large bowl add cake mix, dry pudding mix, eggs, rum, water and oil. Beat on medium speed for 2 minutes. Divide batter equally into two 9-inch cake pans. Bake 25 minutes or until done. Cool, then split each layer in half.

Directions for Filling:

Beat together the milk, rum, dry pudding mix, and whipped topping mix about 4 minutes on high speed. until fluffy. Makes 4 cups. Cover each layer and top of cake with 1 cup of filling. Refrigerate and serve chilled.

Christmas Vanilla Horns

Every Christmas Angie makes these cookies for her brother-in-law David because they are his favorite holiday cookies. They are covered in powdered sugar and melt in your mouth.

Preheat oven to 325°
Ingredients:
1 cup (2 sticks) butter, softened
2/3 cup unsifted powdered sugar
1-1/2 teaspoons vanilla
3/4 cup ground pecans
2 cup unsifted all-purpose flour

Directions:
Beat together butter, sugar and vanilla. Mix well. Add pecans. Stir in flour until well blended. Shape the batter into a ball and place in a bowl covered with wax paper. Refrigerate it one hour.

Lightly grease cookie sheets.

Measure 1 tablespoon of dough for each cookie, roll it into a cylinder, and then bend it to shape it like a crescent moon, and place on cookie sheet.

Bake 10-12 minutes until lightly browned. Cool. Dust with powdered sugar.

Almond Marzipan Candies

Angie and her sisters enjoy creating these candies because they are simple to make and fun to shape and decorate. Depending on the time of the year they might make them into "Summer Fruits" or "Christmas Decorations" or even "Spring Flowers."

Ingredients:
1 package (7oz.) Almond Paste (not Marzipan)
2 cups powdered sugar
3 tablespoons light corn syrup
1/4 teaspoon almond extract
Food colorings
Colored sugars

Directions:
Break up almond paste into a medium size bowl. Stir in 1 cup powdered sugar, corn syrup and almond extract until mixture forms a soft dough, and then continue to stir in enough additional sugar, kneading with hands, until dough is firm enough to hold a shape.

Divide the dough to color and form fruit. (Wrap the dough you aren't working in plastic wrap to keep moist.) Examples:

Peach – light orange food coloring, with yellow and orange sugar sprinkled and a clove for the stem.

Strawberries – red food colorings with red sugar sprinkles. Use a toothpick to make indentations and sprinkle green sugar on the top of berry for leaves.

Place "fruit" on powdered sugar-dusted wax paper or parchment paper to dry. When firm and dry, store in covered containers.

These are so good you might want to double the recipe to make twice as many!

Chocolate Éclairs

This is an elegant looking dessert that Angie likes to serve to guests because the éclairs really are surprisingly easy to make.

Preheat oven to 400°

Ingredients for Choux Pastry:
5 tablespoons butter, diced
2/3 cup water
3/4 cup all-purpose flour, sifted
2 eggs

Ingredients for Pastry Cream:
2 eggs, lightly beaten
4 tablespoons superfine sugar
2 tablespoons cornstarch
1-1/4 cups milk
1/4 teaspoon vanilla extract

Ingredients for Chocolate Icing:
2 tablespoons butter
1 tablespoon milk
1 tablespoon unsweetened cocoa
1/2 cup confectioners' sugar
1-3/4 oz. white chocolate broken into pieces (for swirls on top)

Directions for Choux Pastry:
In saucepan heat the butter and water until the butter is melted. Bring it to a boil then turn heat low and immediately add the flour. Stir fast until dough leaves sides of pan.

Let dough cool then add the eggs. Beat until smooth. Spoon into a large pastry bag fitted with a ½ inch plain tip. Grease a cookie sheet with butter and sprinkle a little water on it. Pipe éclair pastry 4 inches long by 1-1/2 inches wide spaced well apart on the cookie sheet.

Bake for 30-35 minutes at 400 degrees until crisp and golden. Should sound hollow when tapped on the bottom. Place on wire rack to cool.

Directions for Pastry Cream:
In a large bowl whisk together the eggs and sugar until thick then whisk in the cornstarch (be sure to first remove any lumps). Heat the milk in a pan until small bubbles form around the edges (do not boil). Pour the milk onto the egg mixture while whisking. Transfer back to the pan and cook gently, stirring until thick. Remove from heat and stir in the vanilla extract. Cover and cool.

Directions for Chocolate Icing
Melt the butter and milk in a pan. Remove from heat and stir in the cocoa and confectioners' sugar.

Putting it all together
Split the éclairs lengthwise and spoon or pipe in the pastry cream.

Spread the icing over the top of the éclairs.

Heat the white chocolate in a bowl over simmering water until melted. Drizzle it over the dark chocolate icing and let set.

Floating Islands

This classic bistro dessert reminds Angie of the time she was a student at Le Cordon Bleu Paris culinary school, many years ago.

Ingredients for Meringue Islands:
2-1/2 cups skim milk
4 large egg whites
1/4 teaspoon of salt
1/2 cup sugar
1/2 teaspoon vanilla extract

Ingredients for Custard:
4 large egg yolks
1/3 cup sugar
1 teaspoon vanilla extract

Caramel sauce or ground nutmeg for garnish

Directions to make Meringue Islands:

In a saucepan bring milk to a boil, lower heat and simmer.

Using an electric mixer, beat egg whites in large bowl until foamy. Add salt and beat until whites hold soft peaks. Add the sugar, 2 tablespoons at a time, until 1/2 cup has been added, beating until egg whites are stiff and glossy. When all sugar is incorporated, beat 4 to 5 minutes until firm peaks form then beat in vanilla extract until just combined.

Taking a large oval spoon, scoop up some meringue (about the size of a medium lemon), and then, using another large spoon, gently transfer the meringue from spoon to spoon, shaping it into a smooth oval. Drop the oval into milk. Quickly shape

2 or 3 more meringues, dropping each into milk. Poach the meringues 3-5 minutes, turning them over once. They'll puff up while cooking. Use a slotted spoon to move meringues onto a baking sheet lined with paper towels or waxed paper. Repeat process until all meringues are cooked. Refrigerate at least one hour. (Meringues will deflate a bit as they cool..)

Directions to make custard:
Whisk egg yolks with 1/3 cup sugar in a bowl until egg turns thick and pale yellow. Whisk 1/2 cup of the hot milk used with the meringues (reheat it if it has cooled) into egg mixture until blended. Whisk remaining milk in steady stream until smooth.

Return mixture to saucepan and cook over medium-low heat for about 5 minutes stirring constantly until thickened but not boiling. Strain into a clean bowl, cool and then stir in vanilla extract.

To serve:
Ladle 1/2 cup custard into a shallow serving bowl then float 1 to 3 Meringue Islands atop each serving (the number of islands depends on the size of your meringues).

Sprinkle with ground nutmeg and/or drizzle with caramel sauce if you'd like.

Pumpkin Pie with Praline Topping

Angie makes this pie for Thanksgiving.

Preheat oven to 350°

Ingredients for Sweet Cornmeal Crust:
1-1/3 cups flour
3/4 cups yellow cornmeal
1/4 cup packed brown sugar
1/4 teaspoon salt
3/4 cup cold butter
1-3 tablespoons ice water

Ingredients for Pie Filling:
1 can pumpkin (15 oz. size)
1 cup brown sugar
3/4 teaspoon cinnamon
1/2 teaspoon nutmeg
1/2 teaspoon ginger
1/2 teaspoon salt
3 eggs
1 cup half and half
1/3 cup bourbon (optional)

Ingredients for Praline Topping:
3/4 cup brown sugar

1/4 teaspoon nutmeg
1/4 cup butter
2/3 cup chopped pecans

Directions for Crust:
Mix dry ingredients into a bowl and cut in the butter. Add ice water and mix until grainy. Shape into ball and cover in plastic wrap. Refrigerate for 30 minutes, and then pat into pie pan and refrigerate while making the filling.

Directions for Filling:
Beat together all ingredients except half and half and bourbon. Once ingredients are blended slowly add half and half and bourbon until well mixed in. Pour into pie crust bake at 350-degrees for 45-55 minutes until center is firm. Let cool to room temperature.

Directions for Praline Topping:
Mix together then spoon on cool pie. Place under broiler just until topping bubbles. Serve with ice cream or whipped cream if you like.

Cocoa Sauerkraut Cake

A delicious cake, but Angie suggests you keep the strange ingredient a secret!

Preheat oven to 350°
Ingredients for cake
2/3 cup margarine
1-1/2 cup sugar
3 eggs
1 teaspoon vanilla
2-1/4 cups flour, sifted
½ cup cocoa
1 teaspoon baking powder
1 teaspoon baking soda
1/4 teaspoon salt
1 cup cold water
2/3 cup sauerkraut, rinse in cold water, drain, and chopped in small pieces.

Ingredients for frosting
1/2 cube butter
1/3 cup cocoa
¼ cup canned milk
1-2/3 cup powdered sugar
1 teaspoon vanilla

To make the cake: Cream sugar, margarine, eggs together. Add vanilla. Sift in flour, cocoa, baking powder, baking soda, and salt into creamed mixture. Alternate adding cold water and then some sauerkraut into the mix, mix, and continue until all water and sauerkraut added. Pour into two 9-inch cake pans. Bake 350° for 30 minutes.

Mix together all ingredients for frosting and cover two layers of cake. If you prefer thick frosting, double the ingredients (makes a very rich frosting).

Easy Petit Fours

Angie loves pretty things… but making petit fours can be an all-day endeavor. Since she seems to find many other ways to fill her days, she was pleased when she discovered an easy way to make these pretty little cakes.

Preheat oven to 350°

Ingredients for cakes:
1 package of white or yellow cake mix

Ingredients for icing:
9 cups of confectioner's sugar (about 2 lbs.)
1 teaspoon vanilla extract
1/2 teaspoon almond extract
1/2 cup of water
1/2 cup light corn syrup
Food Coloring

Ingredients for Frosting
2 cups confectioner's sugar
1 teaspoon vanilla extract
Enough hot water to make desired consistency to pipe out of decorator bag
Food coloring to tint frosting

Directions for Petit Four Cakes:
Prepare cake mix according to directions on the box. Pour cake mixture into a lightly greased and floured 15 ½" x 10" x 1" jelly-roll pan. Bake 20-25 minutes rotating the pan halfway through to ensure an even bake. Cool in pan for 10 minutes then turn it onto a cooling rack until completely cooled.

Slide cooled cake onto a flat surface and cut into desired shapes--diamonds, hearts, or rounds. Use petit four cookie cutters or just slice into diamonds and squares with knife. Place the cut cake pieces on a wire rack over a clean sheet pan.

Directions for Icing the Petit Fours: The fun part is the decorating! Start by mixing all of the icing ingredients in the top of a double boiler and heat until the ingredients are lukewarm. Remove from the heat but leave the icing over the hot water so it doesn't thicken and turn dry.

Remove a third of the icing and put it in a bowl with a few drops of your choice of food coloring to tint. If the icing becomes cool and thickens, reheat it over the warm water. If the icing is too thin, add more confectioner's sugar.

Pour or ladle the icing over the cake pieces allowing it to run over the sides of the cake. When the icing is completely dry, decorate the tops of the petit fours with Petit Four frosting (below).

PETIT FOUR FROSTING TO DECORATE THE ICING
Pipe out the frosting to look like roses or other flowers, or any shape you like. (Angie usually decorates her petit fours to look like pink, yellow and red roses.)

Place each of the petit fours in a mini paper cupcake cup and store in covered container.

Something Fruit-filled

Cranberry Cream Scones

This simple recipe is Angie's favorite for making scones.

Preheat oven to 400°
Ingredients:
2 cups unsifted all-purpose flour
1/4 cup sugar
1 tablespoon baking powder
Dash salt
1 cup dried cranberries
1-1/4 cups whipping cream
2 tablespoons melted butter
Raw Sugar

Directions:
Stir flour, sugar, baking powder, salt and cranberries together. Add cream. Stir to mix thoroughly, and then knead on floured board 7 or 8 times.

Pat and shape into a circle about 8 inches across. Divide into 8 sections as you would cut a pie.

Grease cookie sheet. Place the scones on the sheet, giving them space to spread. Brush the tops with melted butter and then sprinkle with raw sugar.

Bake at 400 degrees about 18-20 minutes or until lightly browned.

Peach Kuchen

For a dessert that isn't terribly heavy in warm weather, Angie likes to serve peach kuchen with a side of French Vanilla ice cream. It can be made with apples, pears, or berries, but since Paavo is especially fond of peaches, Angie often uses the following recipe for him:

Preheat oven to 350°
Ingredients:
1 package 2-layer size white or yellow cake mix
1/2 cup flaked coconut, toasted
1/2 cup butter
1 can (1 lb 13-oz. size) sliced peaches, drained
2 tablespoons sugar
1/2 teaspoon ground cinnamon
1 cup dairy sour cream
1 slightly beaten egg
Optional: vanilla ice cream on top

Directions:
In a bowl, stir together cake mix and coconut. Soften butter and stir or cut it into dry ingredients. Press onto bottom of 13x9x2-inch pan, and bake at 350° for 10 minutes, until lightly browned.

Drain the peaches and arrange them over the crust, covering as much of the crust as possible. Combine the sugar and cinnamon and then sprinkle the mixture over the peaches. Put sour cream and egg into a small bowl, stir to mix, and then pour it over the crust, peaches, and cinnamon mixture.

Bake about 10 minutes, until the sour cream has set and is firm. Delicious served with vanilla ice cream.

Mom's Apple Pie

Angie's mother makes this pie with vegetable oil instead of butter. The crust turns out flakier than you could imagine.

Preheat oven to 425°

Ingredients for Crust:
3 cups sifted flour
1 teaspoon salt
3/4 cup vegetable oil (Wesson or Crisco Vegetable oil work well)
1/4 cup cold milk

Ingredients for Filling:
5 cups apples, peeled, cored and cut into slices
3/4 cup sugar
1 tablespoon flour
1 teaspoon cinnamon
1/2 teaspoon nutmeg
Pats of butter
1 teaspoon lemon juice

Directions for Crust:
Mix all crust ingredients in a large bowl with a fork. Do not overwork the dough. Divide dough in half and roll into 2 balls. Place 1 ball of dough between wax paper and roll out with rolling pin. Place one crust in a 9 inch pie plate and keep the other as the top crust of pie.

Directions for Filling and Pie:
Combine all filling ingredients in a large bowl. Spoon into pie crust. Put top crust over all and press top and bottom crust together along edges with fork or fingers. Cover the edges with aluminum foil. Bake at 425 degrees for 30 minutes, then remove foil and bake another 10-15 minutes until pie filling is bubbling and crust is golden

brown.

Best Lemon Squares Ever

Angie's parents have a lemon tree in their backyard. Angie likes to use their tree-ripened lemons to bake these lemon squares.

Preheat oven to 350°

Ingredients for crust:
2 cups flour
1/2 cup powdered sugar
1 cup (2 sticks) butter

Ingredients for Topping:
4 eggs
4 tablespoons lemon juice
2 cups sugar
2 tablespoons grated lemon rind
1 tablespoon baking powder
4 tablespoons flour

Directions for Crust:
Make crust by mixing flour, powdered sugar and butter, then pat and press it into a 13 x 9 well-greased pan. Bake at 350 degrees for 15 minutes.

Directions for Topping:
Beat all remaining ingredients together and pour mixture over crust. Bake at 350 degrees for 20-25 min. DO NOT OVERBAKE.

Sift powdered sugar on top while hot.

Pineapple-Cherry Dreams

Angie's mother, Serefina, loves to make these for family gatherings. And they really are dreamy.

Preheat oven to 350°

Ingredients for Cookie Crust:
2 cups flour
1 cup butter
2 tablespoons sugar
1 teaspoon almond extract
1/8 teaspoon salt

Ingredients for Filling:
2 tablespoons cornstarch
1/4 cup cold water
1 can crushed pineapple (8 oz. size)
1/4 cup white sugar
3/4 cup chopped Maraschino cherries

Ingredients for Topping:
2 egg whites
2 tablespoons sugar
1/2 teaspoon almond extract
1/2 cup coconut

Directions for Cookie Crust:
Blend flour, butter, sugar, salt, and almond extract until crumbly. Pat into a 9x9 inch pan. Bake for 20 minutes.

Directions for Filling:
Mix cornstarch with cold water, stir until smooth, breaking up any lumps. Place pineapple and sugar in a saucepan. While it warms, stir in cornstarch-water mixture. Cook until the filling thickens. Allow it to cool, and then add the cherries. Spread filling over baked base.

Directions for Topping:
Beat egg whites with sugar until stiff. Beat in almond extract. Spread over filling and sprinkle with coconut. Bake 25 minutes until medium brown.

Chewy Chocolate-Cherry Cookies

Angie's cousin Leslie gave her this recipe. The cookies are so delicious!

Preheat oven to 350°

Ingredients:
1 cup all-purpose flour
1/3 cup unsweetened cocoa
1/2 teaspoon baking powder
1/4 teaspoon baking soda
1/4 teaspoon salt
1 cup sugar
1/3 cup butter, softened
1 teaspoon vanilla extract
1 large egg
2/3 cup dried tart cherries
3 tablespoons semisweet chocolate chips

Directions:
Using a medium bowl, combine flour, cocoa, baking powder, baking soda and salt. In a large bowl, beat sugar and butter at medium speed until well blended and fluffy. Add vanilla and egg and mix well.

Slowly add flour mixture on slow speed and beat just until combined. Fold in cherries and chocolate chips.

Drop by tablespoons 2 inches apart onto lightly greased cookie sheets. Use butter or cooking spray to grease pans. Bake 12 minutes or just until set.

Cool cookies on pan for 5 minutes and then transfer cookies onto wire racks and cool completely.

Skinny Fig Bars

This recipe is from Angie's cousin Vittoria. She loves to share healthy dessert recipes with Angie—and this one is delicious.

Preheat oven to 350°

Ingredients for Crust:

1 cup flour
1 cup oats (ground)
1 cup almond or flax meal
1/2 teaspoon salt
1/2 cup apple sauce
2 tablespoons coconut oil
3/4 cup coconut sugar
1/2 teaspoon vanilla extract
1/4 cup water
1 egg

Ingredients for Fig Filling:

10 oz. dried figs
4 oz. pitted dates
2 tablespoons honey
3/4 cup brown sugar
3 tablespoons apple butter
1/4 teaspoon anise or vanilla extract
1/4 teaspoon cinnamon
Shredded coconut for topping

Directions for Crust:

Spray 9x9-inch square pan with cooking spray. Combine flour, oats, meal and salt in large bowl. Stir in applesauce, coconut oil, coconut sugar, vanilla and water. Add egg and mix on low speed until blended and thick.

Directions for Fig Filling:
Cut figs and dates and grind in a food processor until it turns into a coarse paste. In a pan on the stove, low-medium heat, add all filling ingredients (except coconut) to the figs and dates. Heat until all is soft. Let cool completely.

Putting it all Together:
Press 1/2 crust mixture into pan (with moist hands). Spread filling evenly over crust.

Smooth the remaining crust over filling. Sprinkle shredded coconut on top.

Bake for 25-30 minutes. Cool completely before cutting into small squares.

Lemon Meringue Tart with Gingersnap Crust

The meringue topping makes this an elegant looking tart. Angie particularly likes to serve this tart when she holds a sit-down dinner party.

Preheat oven to 325°

Ingredients for Crust:
2-1/2 cups crushed gingersnap cookies
2 tablespoons melted butter

Ingredients for Filling:
4 eggs
2 egg yolks
1/2 cup lemon juice
3/4 cup sugar
5 oz. unsalted cold butter, cut into 1/2 inch cubes
Zest of lemons

Ingredients for Meringue:
2/3 cup egg whites, warm (5 egg whites)
1 cup sugar
1/2 teaspoon cream of tartar

Directions for Crust:
Crush the cookies in a food processor or between wax paper with a rolling pin until fine. Stir in melted butter. Press mixture into bottom and sides of 9-inch tart pan. Bake at 325 for 10 to 12 minutes. Set aside.

Directions for Filling:
In a stainless steel bowl, whisk together eggs and egg yolks. Stir in lemon juice and sugar until smooth. Place the bowl over a pan of simmering water and whisk until the mixture thickens. Remove from heat and immediately submerge the bowl in an ice water bath for around 10-15 seconds to stop the cooking process.

Remove from the ice bath and add the butter one piece at a time. Add the lemon zest. Pour the lemon filling into prepared tart pan and bake about 8 minutes until the filing is set.

Directions for Meringue:
Place egg whites, sugar and cream of tartar in a mixer bowl. Whisk the mixture over boiling water until eggs are warmed and the bottom of the bowl is warm to touch. Beat with mixer until stiff and glossy peaks form.

Spread the meringue over the tart covering all around to the edges and shape it to look like a dome. With a spatula or large spoon create peaks by pulling up. Form enough points to cover entire tart.

Place under a broiler for a couple of minutes just until meringue browns or use a kitchen blow torch to brown the meringue lightly all over.

Lite Lemon Bread Pudding & Blackberry Sauce

When Angie's sister, Bianca, was on a diet, Angie made this dessert for her. It's low in calories and fat. They both loved it!

Preheat oven to 350°

Ingredients:
1 cup sugar
1 (16 oz.) pkg. frozen unsweetened blackberries, thawed
2 cups low fat buttermilk
3/4 cups egg substitute (for example, Egg Beaters)
1/3 cup fresh lemon juice
2 tablespoons butter, melted
2 teaspoons grated lemon peel
1/2 pound of French bread (about 8-1 oz. slices) cut into 1-inch cubes
Vegetable cooking spray

Directions:
Combine 1/4 cup sugar and blackberries in container of an electric blender or processor, cover and process until smooth to make blackberry sauce. Set aside.

Combine remaining sugar, buttermilk, egg substitute, lemon juice, butter, lemon peel and bread cubes in a large bowl and toss gently to mix.
Let stand for 1 hour.

Lightly cover 11x7x2-inch baking dish with cooking spray. Spoon mixture into it and bake at 350° for 40 minutes until set. Serve with blackberry sauce.

Cherry Coconut Birthday Cupcakes

Birthdays are always special, but for a change of pace, Angie sometimes makes cupcakes instead of cake.

Preheat oven to 350°

Ingredients for Cake:
8 tablespoons butter, softened
1/2 cup superfine sugar
2 tablespoons milk
2 eggs
1/2 cup self-rising flour
1/2 teaspoon baking powder
3/4 dry unsweetened coconut
4 oz. candied cherries, quartered

Ingredients for Buttercream:
1 cup butter
1 tablespoons cream or milk
3 cups confectioners' sugar (sifted)

Directions for Cake:
Line 12 muffin tins with paper liners. Beat together butter and sugar in a large bowl until fluffy. Stir in the milk and then beat in the eggs. Sift flour and baking powder and fold them in with the coconut. Gently fold in most of the quartered cherries. Spoon into the paper cups and scatter remaining cherries on top.

Bake for 20-25 minutes or until golden brown and firm to the touch. Cool completely before frosting.

Directions for Buttercream:
Place the butter and cream in a bowl and beat until fluffy. Slowly add the sifted confectioners' sugar and beat until smooth.

Frost the cupcakes once they have cooled and decorate with whole candied, maraschino, or fresh cherries.

Exquisite Raspberry Tart

When fresh raspberries are in season, Angie loves to make this tart. It's time consuming, but rave reviews make it well worth the effort.

Preheat oven to 350°
Ingredients for Walnut Butter Pastry:
1/2 cup butter (room temperature)
2-1/2 tablespoons sugar
1/2 cup finely chopped walnuts
1 egg (beaten)
1 teaspoon almond extract

1-1/3 cup flour

Ingredients for Vanilla Custard Filling:
2 egg yolks (room temperature)
2 1/2 tablespoons sugar
2 tablespoons cornstarch
1/2 teaspoon vanilla extract
2/3 cup milk
6 tablespoons butter (room temperature)

Ingredients for Topping:
4 cups fresh raspberries
1 cup red currant jelly
1 cup whipping cream

Directions for Pastry:
Butter 10 or 11-inch springform pan. Cream 1/2 cup butter and sugar in large bowl. Mix in walnuts. Blend in egg and almond extract. Stir in flour. Press dough in pan.

Refrigerate 30 minutes. Bake at 350 degrees until golden brown 15-20 mins. Cool to room temp.

Directions for Vanilla Custard Filling:
Beat egg yolks, sugar, cornstarch and vanilla in medium bowl until pale and thick. Heat milk in heavy saucepan. Beat milk into yolk mixture until smooth. Return mixture to saucepan and whisk over medium heat until very thick about 5 minutes. Return to bowl and beat until cool. Beat in butter, one tablespoon at a time. Refrigerate until chilled.

Directions to Assemble Tart:
Spread custard evenly over crust.

Starting from the outside edge, place berries over custard. Refrigerate for 30 minutes. Melt red currant jelly in heavy saucepan over low heat stirring occasionally. Brush over berries gently, covering completely.

Refrigerate at least 2 hours before serving. Serve with whipped cream.

Chocolate Torte with Apricot Filling

Espresso powder intensifies the chocolate flavor of the smooth shiny frosting. Angie likes the added kick of spices in this cake, but you can leave them out if you prefer your chocolate cake "straight".

Preheat oven to 350°

Ingredients for Cake:

6 large eggs
3/4 cup sugar
1 teaspoon vanilla extract
1/2 cup plus 1 tablespoon sifted all-purpose flour
1/2 cup sifted unsweetened cocoa powder
1 teaspoon ground allspice
1 teaspoon ground cinnamon
1/4 teaspoon ground nutmeg

Ingredients for Frosting and Filling:

1-1/2 cups part-skim ricotta cheese
1/4 cup plus 2 tablespoons unsweetened cocoa powder
2 tablespoons instant espresso powder
3 tablespoons sugar
2 teaspoons vanilla extract
1/8 teaspoon salt
3/4 cup apricot all-fruit spread
Strawberries for garnish (optional)

Directions for Cake:

Spray two 8-inch round cake pans with cooking spray. In a large electric mixer bowl at high speed, beat the eggs, sugar and vanilla until thick and tripled in volume (5-7 minutes).

In medium bowl sift together dry ingredients, flour, cocoa powder, allspice, cinnamon and nutmeg. Using a large rubber spatula, gently fold the dry ingredients into the egg mixture until smooth. Divide the mixture between the two prepared pans.

Bake about 15 minutes. Check if done by inserting a toothpick in center of cake to see if it comes out clean. Cool completely in the pans on racks.

Directions for Frosting and Filling:
In a food processor or blender, process the ricotta cheese, cocoa powder, espresso powder, sugar, vanilla and salt until smooth. Cover and chill until ready to use.

When the cake is cool, split each layer in half horizontally and spread the bottom half of each layer with half of the apricot all-fruit spread. Carefully replace top layers.

Spread half of the frosting evenly over the top of one of the filled layers. Stack second layer on top of the first. Swirl remaining frosting evenly over the top of the cake. Garnish with whole strawberries if desired.

Something Nutty

Almond Praline Meringue Layer Cake

Angie's mother loved making this delicious cake for special occasions, and now Angie does the same. It's especially popular at Easter Brunch gatherings.

Preheat oven to 350°.

Ingredients for Praline:
1/2 cup blanched almonds
1/2 cup sugar
3 tablespoons water

Ingredients for Meringue:
1-2 tablespoons soft butter
1/4 cup flour
6 oz. ground blanched almonds
1 cup sugar
1 1/2 tablespoons cornstarch
6 egg whites
1/8 teaspoon salt
1/4 teaspoon cream of tartar
3 tablespoons sugar
1 1/2 teaspoons vanilla extract
1/8 teaspoon almond extract

Ingredients for Butter Cream and Chocolate Frosting
1 cup sugar
6 egg yolks
3/4 cup hot milk
12 oz. (3 cubes) unsalted butter
1 teaspoon vanilla extract
3 tablespoons Kirsch (or dark rum or strong coffee)
2 oz. unsweetened baking chocolate, melted

Directions to make Praline:
Preheat oven to 350°. To make the praline, spread almonds on baking sheet and roast at for 10-15 minutes until brown. Stir several times. Combine sugar and water and set over medium high heat. Stir occasionally as liquid boils and turns thick. When sugar is caramel brown, remove from heat, add almonds, mix and turn onto lightly oiled

tray. When cold and hard (about 20 minutes) break up and grind in electric blender.

Directions for Meringue:

Turn down oven to 250°. Rub butter over two large baking sheets, then smooth flour over them. Using an 8-inch cake pan or pot lid, make three 8-inch rings on sheets by placing the pan on the sheet and marking around edges with tip of rubber spatula. Set aside.

Mix together almonds, sugar and cornstarch. Set aside.

Beat egg whites until foamy. Add salt and cream of tartar and beat to soft peaks. Add sugar, vanilla and almond and continue to beat until egg whites form stiff peaks.

Using about 1/4 of almond-sugar mixture at a time, rapidly fold into egg whites, deflating eggs as little as possible. Use pastry bag or spatula to place egg mixture into areas marked on baking sheets. Bake about 30-40 minutes at 250°. They will not grow or puff up, but will lightly brown and are done when can be pushed loose from baking surface.

Directions for Butter Cream and Chocolate Frosting

In heavy saucepan, beat sugar and egg yolks until thick, pale yellow. Gradually stir in hot milk and set over medium heat. Stir 4-5 minutes until thick enough to coat spoon but not to a simmer. Remove from heat. Quickly add butter a little at a time, stirring to melt and absorb. Last, mix in vanilla and Kirsch.

Remove 1/4 of mixture. Add chocolate to it and set aside.

Add almond praline (from above praline directions) to remaining (3/4) of butter cream.

Putting it all together:

Build cake by placing one meringue on a cake rack. Cover with 1/3 of butter cream. Add second meringue and spread 1/2 of remaining butter cream on it. Cover with final meringue. Spread remaining butter cream over sides of cake. Spread chocolate frosting over top of cake.

Almond Butter Cake with Crunchy Almond Topping

If there was ever a dessert recipe you must try, it's this one. Your guests will be sure you bought it in a bakery (and paid a pretty penny for it). Only Angie and you will know how very simple it is to make.

Preheat oven to 350°

Ingredients:
1-1/2 cups sugar (plus 2 teaspoons for topping)
3/4 cup (1-1/2 sticks) butter, melted
2 eggs
2 teaspoons almond extract
1-1/2 cups all-purpose flour
3/4 cup sliced almonds

Directions:
Stir 1 1/2 cups sugar and butter in a large bowl. Stir in eggs and almond extract. Blend in flour. Pour in greased 9-inch pan (a springform pan works especially well). Sprinkle with 2 teaspoons sugar and sliced almonds over the top.

Bake at 350° for 40 minutes until golden. Cake might not test clean with a toothpick, but don't overcook. Slice fairly thin—it's rich!

Mocha Pecan Torte

Angie knows her tortes, and this one is her absolute favorite. It's wonderfully rich, made with only a little flour and lots of ground pecans, coming as close to perfection as ever a torte can be.

Preheat oven to 350°

Ingredients:
3 tablespoons sifted all-purpose flour
1 teaspoon baking powder
12 oz. pecans, finely ground
6 eggs, separated
2 tablespoons instant coffee powder
1-1/2 cups sugar
1/8 teaspoon salt
Dry bread crumbs

Ingredients for Icing and Filling:
3 oz. (6 tablespoons) butter
4 oz. unsweetened chocolate
1 tablespoon plus 1 teaspoon instant coffee powder
2 cups confectioners' sugar
1/3 cup milk
2 eggs
1 teaspoon vanilla extract

Directions:
Butter two 9-inch cake pans and dust with dry bread crumbs or flour, or cover bottoms with parchment paper, or use springform pans (torte batter tends to stick to pans).

Place ground pecans in a large bowl. Sift flour and baking powder over pecans, stir to mix. Set side.

In a medium-size bowl, beat egg yolks at high speed for three minutes. Reduce speed while gradually adding instant coffee powder and sugar. Increase speed to high and beat 5 minutes until very thick. Stir in ground pecan mixture. Set aside.

Using clean beaters and a bowl, beat egg whites with salt until stiff but not dry. Using about a quarter of the whites at a time, gently fold them into the eggs-nut-flour mixture until blended.

Divide the mixture equally between the two prepared cake pans. Bake 35-40 minutes. Cakes are done when the top springs back when lightly touched and the sides begin to pull away from the pan. Let cool 10 minutes, then remove from pans.

Directions for Icing and Filling:
Using a microwave or double boiler, melt chocolate, and then add butter and stir until melted. Add instant coffee and stir to dissolve. Set aside to cool.

Mix sugar, milk, eggs, and vanilla in a bowl. Place the bowl in a larger bowl half filed with ice and cold water. Add cooled chocolate mixture and beat at high speed 3-4 minutes until fluffy and light in color.

Directions for Putting the Torte Together:
Place four thin strips of wax paper or aluminum foil to cover edge of cake plate. Place one cake layer upside down on the plate. Spread filling half an inch thick on it. Cover with the second cake layer, right side up. Spread icing on top and sides of torte. Carefully remove wax paper (or foil).

Refrigerate 2-3 hours before serving.

Pistachio Pudding Bars

Popular years ago, Angie's mother, Serefina, used to make this dessert often. The butter cookie crust and light texture topping are delicious!

Preheat oven to 375°

Ingredients for Crust:
2 cups flour
1/2 cup butter, softened
1/2 cup ground almonds

Ingredients for Filling:
2 pkg. Pistachio Instant Pudding mix
3 cups milk
1 teaspoon vanilla

Ingredients for Topping:
8 oz. cream cheese, softened
1 cup Cool Whip
1 cup confectioners' sugar

Directions for Crust:
Combine flour, butter, almonds in a bowl. Press into a 9x13 pan. Bake 15 minutes.

Directions for Filling:
Beat together pudding mix, milk and vanilla. Spread over cooled cookie crust.

Directions for Topping:
Beat together until mixed well. Use a wet knife or spatula to spread over filling. Keep refrigerated until ready to serve.

Linzer Torte

This lattice-topped torte features an almond pastry and jam filling.

Preheat oven to 325°
Ingredients:
1-1/2 cups flour
1/2 cup ground blanched almonds
1/2 teaspoon ground cinnamon
1/4 teaspoon salt
1/4 teaspoon baking powder

1/2 cup sugar

1/4 cup tub-style light cream cheese
1/2 teaspoon vanilla extract
1 large egg
Cooking spray
1 1/4 cup seedless blackberry, raspberry or apricot jam
1 teaspoon confectioners' sugar

Directions:
Combine flour, almonds, cinnamon, salt and baking powder in a bowl.

In a food processor, combine sugar and cream cheese in a food processor, mix. Add vanilla and egg, and then mix. Add the flour mixture and pulse until combined. The dough will be sticky. Cover 2/3 of the dough in two sheets of plastic wrap. Chill for 30 minutes.

Gently press remaining 1/3 of dough into 4-inch circle on   heavy duty plastic wrap and cover with additional plastic wrap. Roll into a 9-inch circle. Chill for 30 minutes. Roll the larger portion of dough into an 11-inch circle and chill for 10 minutes or until the plastic wrap can be easily removed.

Working with the larger portion of dough, remove the top sheet of plastic wrap, fit dough into a greased 9-inch round removable bottom pan with low sides (used for tarts and tortes). Remove top sheet of plastic wrap. Fold edges under. Spoon the jam into prepared crust.

Working with the smaller portion of dough, remove top sheet of plastic wrap. Cut dough into ½- inch strips. Remove strips from bottom sheet of plastic, arrange in a lattice design over preserves. Seal dough strips to the edge of crust.

Place torte on baking sheet and bake for 50 minutes until the crust is brown and the filling is bubbly. Cool on wire rack. Sprinkle with confectioners' sugar.

Bourbon Pecan Chocolate Pie

Combining pecan and chocolate into a pie, and topping the mixture with bourbon, is sure to delight. It's one of Angie's favorite pies.

Preheat oven to 350°
Ingredients:
1 cup coarsely chopped pecans
4 eggs
1/2 cup light corn syrup
1/4 cup honey
1/3 cup sugar
1/3 cup packed light brown sugar
6 tablespoons unsalted butter, melted
3 tablespoons bourbon
1 tablespoon vanilla
1 tablespoon all-purpose flour
pinch ground nutmeg
pinch ground cinnamon
8 ounces bittersweet chocolate
pastry for 1 crust pie

Directions:
Toast the pecans in a small skillet over medium-high heat, stirring often until they are evenly toasted and crisp, about 4 minutes. (Note: you can substitute walnuts, or use half pecans and half walnuts.) Set aside to cool.

In a bowl, add eggs, corn syrup, honey, sugar, brown sugar, butter, bourbon, vanilla, flour, nutmeg and cinnamon. Whisk or blend until mixture is smooth. Break chocolate into one-half inch square chunks. Stir chocolate and nuts into mix. Pour into uncooked pie crust and bake at 350 degrees until set, 40-50 minutes. Serve warm.

Zucchini Bread

Being Italian means planting zucchini every summer. Angie's grandparents always had an abundance of it growing in the garden. There is just so much zucchini one can eat...but zucchini bread is another matter!

Preheat oven to 350°
Ingredients:
2 cups sugar
3 eggs, beaten
1 cup oil
3 cups flour
2 teaspoons cinnamon
1 teaspoon baking soda
1 teaspoon salt
1 teaspoon baking powder
2 teaspoons vanilla
3-1/2 cups shredded zucchini (2 large or 3-4 medium)
1-1/2 cups chopped walnuts

Directions:
Mix all the ingredients in a large bowl.

Put in two 5x9 loaf pans which have been greased with butter.

Bake for 1 hour. These freeze well.

Heavenly Carrot-Walnut Cake & Cream Cheese Frosting.

This carrot cake is so filled with healthy ingredients, Angie sometimes bakes it in loaf pans, leaves off the frosting and serves it with breakfast or brunch.

Preheat oven to 350°

Ingredients for Cake:

3 cups flour, sifted
2 cups sugar
1-1/2 teaspoon baking soda
2 teaspoons cinnamon
1 teaspoon baking powder
1-1/2 teaspoon salt
1/2 cup vegetable oil
1 can pineapple (8-3/4oz. size)—separate juice and fruit
2 teaspoons vanilla extract
3 eggs
2 cups grated carrots
2 cups walnuts nuts

Ingredients for Cream Cheese Frosting:

8 oz. cold cream cheese
1 stick unsalted butter, firm but not cold
1/8 teaspoon salt
3 3/4 cups confectioners' sugar, sifted
1/2 teaspoon vanilla extract

Directions for Cake:
In a large bowl, add flour, sugar, baking soda, cinnamon, baking powder and salt. Add oil, juice from pineapple., vanilla extract, and eggs. Beat until well blended. Stir in carrots, pineapple fruit, and nuts. Pour into 2 greased 9-inch round pans. Bake 25-30 minutes until toothpick comes out clean when inserted into middle of cake. Cool cake completely before frosting.

Directions for Frosting:
Beat cream cheese, butter and salt on medium speed until creamy. Reduce the speed to low and gradually add the confectioners' sugar until incorporated. Add the vanilla and beat just until mixed in. Do not over beat. The frosting should be creamy and

dense. Add milk, 1 teaspoon at a time if the frosting is not spreadable.

Almond Divinity Candy

Angie's sister's mother-in-law, Kaye, used to make this heavenly candy.

Ingredients:
2 cups sugar
1/2 cup white corn syrup
1/2 cup water
2 egg whites
1 teaspoon vanilla
1/2 cup of chopped almonds

Directions:
Place sugar, corn syrup and water in a saucepan over low heat. Stir until the sugar is dissolved, then cook without stirring to 252 degrees (until a little dropped into cold water forms a hard ball).

Place two egg whites in bowl with electric mixer. Remove the sugar mixture from the heat and pour it in a fine stream, mixing constantly, into the egg whites. Mix on high speed until stiff. Continue beating until mixture holds its shape and loses its gloss.

Add vanilla and nuts. Drop quickly from tip of spoon into individual peaks onto waxed paper or spread in a greased shallow pan and cut into 1 inch squares when firm.

Cardamom Icebox Cookies

These are a delicious spicy cookie for wintertime, and the dough keeps nicely in the freezer for when guests drop by unexpectedly.

Preheat oven to 375 °
Ingredients:
4 cups unsifted all-purpose flour
1-1/2 teaspoon baking soda
1 tablespoon ground cardamom
1 cup butter (2 sticks)
3/4 cup sugar
3/4 cup firmly packed light brown sugar
3 eggs
1 cup walnuts or pecans, finely chopped

Directions:
Sift together flour, baking soda and cardamom into a small bowl. In a large mixer bowl, beat butter, sugar and brown sugar until well mixed. Add eggs, one at a time. Stir in flour mixture gradually until well blended. Stir in nuts.

Divide dough into 4 equal parts. Shape into logs that are about 10 inches long. Roll each log in waxed paper. Chill overnight or for several hours so they are firm enough to slice. (Cookie dough logs may be frozen at this time, by using plastic wrap to tightly cover each wax paper wrapped log.) Cut logs into 1/2 inch slices and place on greased cookie sheets about 2 inches apart.

Bake 10 minutes or so until the cookies are lightly browned.

Cool on wire racks. Store in tightly covered container.

Almond Rose Cookies

Covered in powder sugar these cookies are crunchy on the outside and chewy on the inside.

Preheat oven to 350°

Ingredients:
2 cups ground almonds
2-1/2 teaspoons baking powder
1 teaspoon cinnamon
3 tablespoons rosewater*
1/2 teaspoon almond extract
Zest of 1 orange
1-1/2 cups confectioners' sugar
1 egg, lightly beaten

Directions:
Mix ground almonds, baking powder, cinnamon, rosewater, almond extract, orange zest and 1 cup (set aside the remaining 1/2 cup) of confectioners' sugar in a mixing bowl. Add the lightly beaten egg and stir well until the dough is firm.

Pour the remaining 1/2 cup of confectioners' sugar into a shallow dish. Wet your hands (to prevent the dough from sticking on them) and roll 1 teaspoon dough in to balls.

Roll the balls in the confectioners' sugar until heavily coated then place on a greased or non-stick cookie sheet and gently flatten.

Bake 15 minutes. Let cool 10 minutes on the cookie sheet before transferring to a wire rack to cool completely.

*if rosewater isn't available, substitute 1 teaspoon vanilla extract and 2-1/2 tablespoons plain water.

"Hello Dolly" Cookies

Many years ago, Angie's sister, Bianca, made these cookies, entered them in a bake contest and won! These are layered in a unique way so they are very moist.

Preheat oven to 350°
Ingredients:
3/4 cube butter
1 cup graham cracker crumbs
1 cup coconut (sweetened flake type)
1 cup semi-sweet chocolate chips
1 cup chopped walnuts
1 can Eagle brand sweetened condensed milk

Directions:
Melt the butter in an 8x8-inch square pan then add the graham cracker crumbs. Push down in pan.

Add in layers: coconut on the bottom, chocolate chips, and then walnuts. Pour 1 can sweetened condensed milk over all.

Bake for 30 minutes. Cool then cut into squares.

INDEX

Almond Butter Cake with Crunchy Almond Topping 93
Almond Divinity Candy 104
Almond Marzipan Candies 52
Almond Praline Meringue Layer Cake 90
Almond Rose Cookies 106
Angie's Easy Tiramisu 14
Best Lemon Squares Ever 70
Biscotti di Prato (Tuscan Almond Biscotti) 28
Bourbon Pecan Chocolate Pie 100
Cannoli 16
Cardamom Icebox Cookies 105
Cherry Coconut Birthday Cupcakes 82
Chewy Chocolate-Cherry Cookies 74
Chocolate Éclairs 54
Chocolate Rum Cake 49
Chocolate Soufflé 40
Chocolate Torte with Apricot Filling 86
Christmas Vanilla Horns 50
Cocoa Sauerkraut Cake 61
Cranberry Cream Scones 66
Easy Petit Fours 62
Exquisite Raspberry Tart 84
Floating Islands 57
French Macarons 42

Greek Butter Cookies (Kourabiedes) 45

Heavenly Carrot-Walnut Cake & Cream Cheese Frosting. 102

"Hello Dolly" Cookies.. 108

Iced Italian Wedding Cookies 26

Italian Cheese Pie 34

Italian Honey Cookies 37

Italian Napoleons 18

Italian Style Chocolate-Amaretto Bread Pudding 22

Lemon Meringue Tart with Gingersnap Crust 78

Linzer Torte 98

Lite Chocolate Amaretto Cheesecake... 24

Lite Lemon Bread Pudding & Blackberry Sauce 81

Mocha Pecan Torte.. 94

Mom's Apple Pie 69

Orange-Cinnamon Biscotti 30

Ossi Di Morti Cookies (Bones of the Dead) 21

Peach Kuchen... 68

Pineapple-Cherry Dreams 72

Pistachio Pudding Bars 96

Pumpkin Pie with Praline Topping... 59

Skinny Fig Bars.. 76

Snickerdoodles 46

Ultimate Cheesecake... 48

Zabaglione.. 32

Zeppole... 38

Zucchini Bread 101

Joanne Pence is an award-winning, *USA Today* best-selling author of mysteries, supernatural suspense, historical fiction, romance and fantasy. Born and raised in the San Francisco Bay Area, she now makes her home in the foothills overlooking Boise, Idaho. Joanne hopes you'll enjoy her books, which present a variety of times, places, and reading experiences, from mysterious to thrilling, emotional to lightly humorous, as well as powerful tales of times long past. Visit her at JoannePence.com, and be sure to sign up for her New Release mailing list.

Loretta Barra, Emmy award winner for her electronic graphics work at the 1984 Summer Olympics, discovered she enjoys painting with watercolors when she took her first watercolor class at Rancho La Puerta in Tecate Mexico, over ten years ago. Since then she has taken a number of classes and workshops from leading artists. Her work won first place at the City of Moraga's Pear & Wine Festival, and has been on display at a number of venues in California and Idaho. She is a member of the California Watercolor Association, and the Idaho Watercolor Association. Look for her whimsical paintings on RedBubble.com and Zazzle.com under ArtSweets.

www.ingramcontent.com/pod-product-compliance
Lightning Source LLC
Chambersburg PA
CBHW081336080526
44588CB00017B/2646